Skira Guides

Skira Guides

Pietro C. Marani

Leonardo da Vinci's Last Supper

Front cover
Leonardo da Vinci, *The Last Supper*
From the left, the figures of Judas Iscariot, Peter and John (detail)

Facing title page
Interior view of the refectory of Santa Maria delle Grazie

Editor
Eileen Romano

Design
Marcello Francone

Editorial coordination
Giovanna Rocchi

Editing
Maria Conconi

Layout
Anna Cattaneo

Iconographical Research
Marta Tosi

Translation
Darcy Di Mona
for Scriptum, Rome

First published in Italy in 2009
by Skira Editore S.p.A.
Palazzo Casati Stampa
via Torino 61
20123 Milano
Italy

Many thanks to Ivana Novani of the Milan Architectural Superintendency for her invaluable assistance.

Photographic credits
Photographs by M. Gavinelli, V. Mirarchi, A. Temporelli, © HAL9000 Srl Novara, Italy, www.haltadefinizione.com, by permission of the Ministero per i Beni e le Attività Culturali, Soprintendenza per i Beni Architettonici e Paesaggistici di Milano [Ministry of Cultural Heritage, Superintendency of Landscape and Architectural Heritage for Milan]
Soprintendenza per i Beni Architettonici e per il Paesaggio per le province di Milano, Bergamo, Como, Lecco, Lodi, Pavia, Sondrio e Varese [Superintendency of Landscape and Architectural Heritage for the provinces of Milan, Bergamo, Como, Lecco, Lodi, Pavia, Sondrio and Varese]
© The Royal Collection, Her Majesty Queen Elisabeth II, Windsor

Printed and bound in Italy.
First edition

ISBN 978-88-572-0447-5

www.skira.net

Contents

1. Entrance
2. Leonardo, *The Last Supper*
3. Donato Montorfano, *The Crucifixion*
4. Refectory with *The Last Supper*
5. Major cloister
6. Santa Maria delle Grazie
7. Ticket office and reception
8. Bookshop
9. Facilities

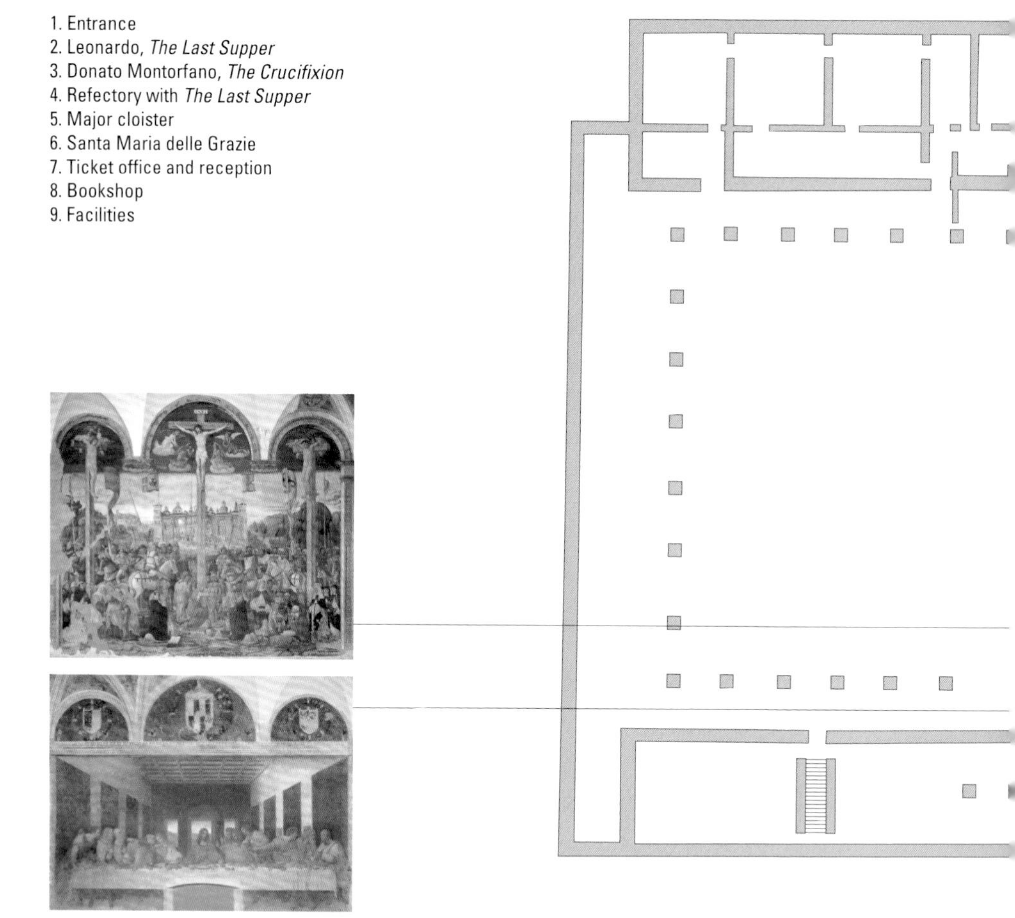

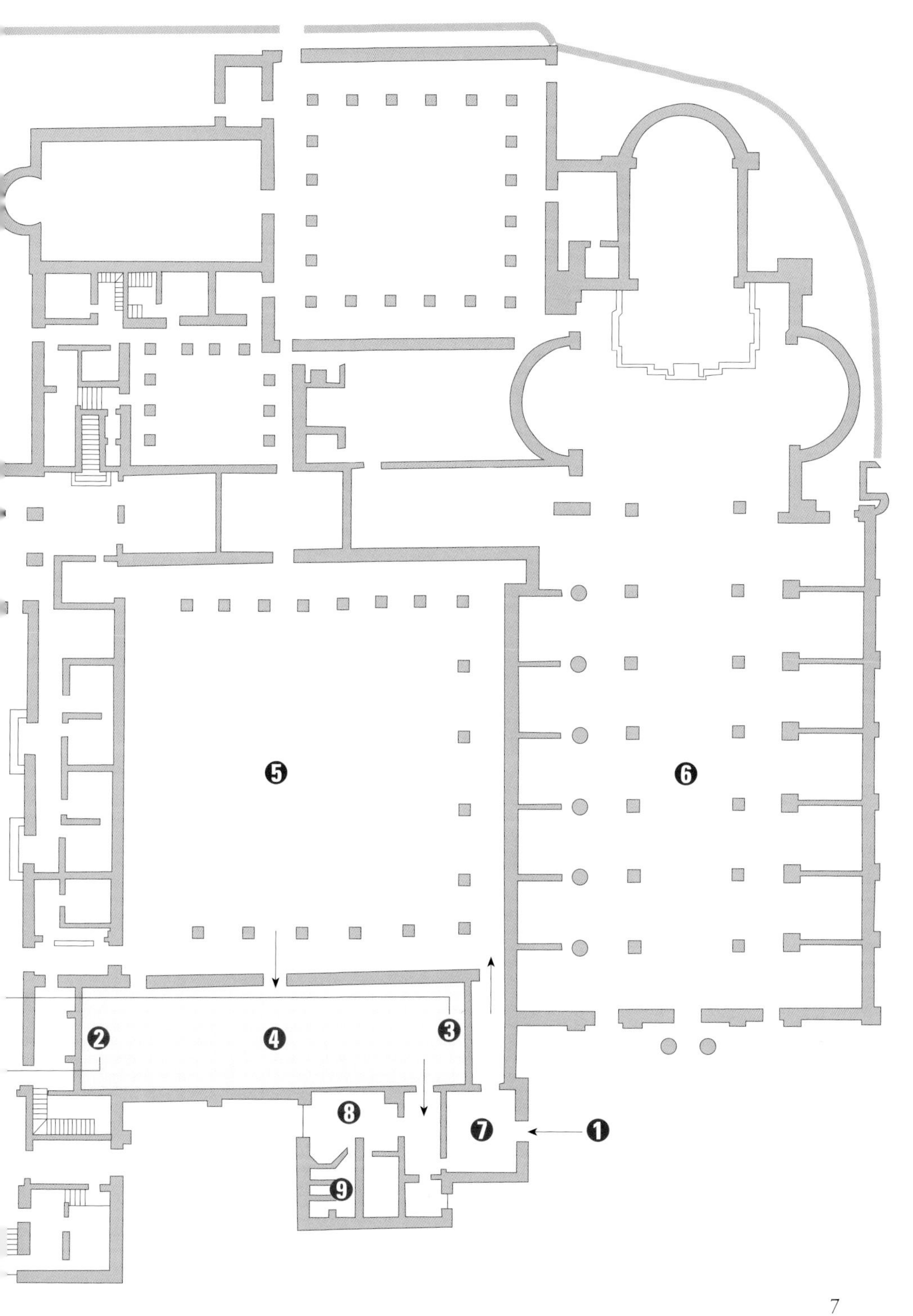
1
2
3
4
5
6
7
8
9

Preface to the new edition

The restoration of Leonardo's *Last Supper*, carried out between 1977 and 1999, surely represents a turning point in the methodology of mural painting restoration, and perhaps in the history of art restoration as well. It went steadily ahead despite difficulties and problems of every conceivable kind, from the fear of even approaching such a famous artwork, to the paradox of trying to conserve and "restore" a painting that history had already bequeathed to us in an altered and tampered state, to the point that only the "shadow" of Leonardo's lost masterpiece remains today; finally, but hardly less significant, there was the matter of the relationship between the restoration effort and the iconic image that had taken root in the viewers' consciousness and visual imagination for at least a century.

Today, exactly ten years after its completion, the complex process of saving the painting is ready, in 2009, for a verification of its results and their durability over time. The approval of critics in Italy and the world over, and the unending stream of visitors from the four corners of the globe to Milan to see what is still, perhaps, universally the most famous mural painting in art history, would certainly seem to buttress the conviction that back in 1977 the right decisions were made, in terms of aesthetic and conservation concerns, by the Superintendent for Artistic and Historical Heritage in Milan, along with the Istituto Centrale per il Restauro and the many international scientific institutions that provided their support and collaboration for the duration of the project.

Begun on Stella Matalan's initiative as an emergency intervention after fragments of the painting flaked off in 1977, the actual restoration campaign, spearheaded by Carlo Bertelli, got off to a timely and intelligent start in the years immediately following, under the super-

Leonardo da Vinci, *The Last Supper* The figure of Philip (detail).

vision of Pinin Brambilla Barcilon, with her extraordinary sensibility. In the early 80s visitors could already appreciate the quality of her first findings and, above all, the unexpected beauty and variety of the original colours that had survived under the crust of paint from repaintings and touch-ups in the modern era. Subsequently, under the successive supervision of Rosalba Tardito, Pietro Petraroia, and Bruno Contardi (and in association with the present author since 1992), more and more new elements came to light, which made the work's original form, the structure and composition, and the understanding of the space between figures much more legible.
The restoration process was extremely delicate. When we started out, we certainly did not intend or even remotely dream of making Leonardo's painting look exactly the way the artist had left it when he finally laid down his brush. Our main concern was to conserve the original layers of pigment we knew had survived the five centuries of its tortuous history; indeed, our findings far exceeded our expectations in terms of quality and quantity. As we have said above, not only has the painting come down to us in an altered form, due to the effects of time and the trials it has undergone; our very image of the work is distorted by the accumulation of past critical interpretations of the painting, the various copies other artists made of it, and, last but not least, the image of it that our collective consciousness had come to adopt. Thus, while the restoration has unveiled fragments that still show their great age and bear the "signs" of passing time (the historical significance of the painting, if you will), the fact remains that the visitor does need to make a mental leap to connect the restored version with the "idea" long formed in his mind (thanks to inexpensive reproductions and photographs that are instantly available, all of which are retouched and altered to provide as complete an image of the picture as possible).
Interspaced as it is with large areas where nothing of the original survives, there is no doubt that the painting is fragmentary. However, these very fragments, with their intense, bright colours, are now interwoven by means of very cautious, pale-hued, water-colour additions (so as to make it always clear where the original painting finishes and where the areas in which it has been irremediably lost begin). The result is a more reliable image, one that is closer to the lost original than the almost total repaintings of the eighteenth century, which not only altered and distorted the figures' faces, expressions and attitudes, along with the colours; for over two hundred years, those early restoration attempts also managed to conceal the general effect of the composition. They removed any suggestion of depth, and,

more importantly, made no attempt to preserve the perfectly balanced play of light and shadow that gives the newly restored painting, "reborn" as the sum of its fragments, that tonal equilibrium by means of which Leonardo had successfully solved the problem of the relationship between *chiaroscuro* and colour.

The text presented here as the first guide to unlocking Leonardo's masterpiece was written in 1986 (and published by Electa in the same year), at the very moment when we were wildly enthusiastic over the first sensational discoveries, which I witnessed firsthand, as I was working for the Superintendent for Artistic and Historical Heritage in Milan. It was also the time, however, when it seemed necessary to approach the painting with the aid of new critical tools that took into account the interpretations that had been proposed by art historians especially in Great Britain, such as Ernst H. Gombrich and Martin Kemp, not to mentions Italians like Anna Maria Brizio and Carlo Pedretti, who tended to place the genesis of *The Last Supper* squarely in the context of Leonardo's scientific speculations and inquiry.

What emerged was a reading of the work that definitively forsook the rhetorical, celebratory tone that had distinguished art criticism between the two World Wars and instead reaffirmed the status of Leonardo's painting as the highest expression of that link between art and science that characterises all his work, and, above all, reiterated its role as a virtual "manifesto" of his artistic conceptions. The reader may therefore deem this early, "youthful" attempt at a guide overly ambitious and even a bit superficial in its desire to condense – in a few introductory remarks meant to facilitate the approach to Leonardo's masterpiece – the results of studies that the present author has elaborated in later works, especially in his book published in 1999 and co-written with Pinin Brambilla herself, which constitutes the effective "publication" of the twenty-odd-year-long restoration of the wall painting, and amounts to a "final report" over four hundred pages long! I have, however, decided against altering the content of the original guide, intended, after all, as a visitor's initial approach, and one historically oriented, to this famous mural painting. The entire first part of the guide (a reconstruction of the painting's history and significance) has thus undergone little change, whereas the last part has required a number of corrections and additions, insofar as it refers to the results of the restoration, which at the time of the first writing was still in progress. Needless to say, this painstaking restoration project was also affected by the fact that it took so many years to complete, over the course of which there were noticeable changes in direction and methodology (though not in the high standard of the philological re-

search that had inspired it from the start). Since these changes are reflected in the reports and studies that have appeared in tandem with the restoration, a bibliography has now been added to provide the interested reader with further information.
For example, in a very recent re-examination of the stratigraphy, the restoration has at long last confirmed an all-important material aspect of the work: the choice of medium Leonardo employed. Thanks to chemical and physical analyses on paint samples, there is no longer any doubt that tempera was used and was applied to two layers of chalky plaster, perhaps along with a thin layer of oil in a few places. Moreover, as far as the perspective scheme adopted by Leonardo is concerned, the rediscovery of the lines he incised in the upper left portion of the composition, and the definitive interpretation of the section on the extreme right, after the first tapestry, as a stretch of wall shown in perspective, are the demonstration that what the artist reproduced was an imaginary room wider than the actual refectory, his intention being to provide a more illusionistic background than was earlier believed, from which the table and the figures of Christ and the apostles could project three-dimensionally.

Leonardo da Vinci's Last Supper

Leonardo's early ideas for *The Last Supper*, or *Cenacolo*, in Santa Maria delle Grazie in Milan, are illustrated in a sheet of figure studies, no. 12542r, conserved in the Royal Library at Windsor Castle[1]. It features five figure studies in all, the largest of which, at the top of the sheet, shows eight or nine disciples grouped around Christ, with Judas seated on the side of the table nearest the viewer. The backdrop is a wall broken at regular intervals by corbel vaults, in which a row of lunettes is set; in fact, this corresponds to the actual design of the long walls of the refectory of Santa Maria delle Grazie, although there is absolutely no evidence that Leonardo intended to paint *The Last Supper* on one of these walls, which would have called for enormous figures.
With its vigorous, darting pen strokes, the Windsor drawing of the largest group is purposefully concise: facial features are barely suggested, with blots and crossed dashes marking noses and eyebrows. The second drawing on the sheet, on the right-hand side and on a slightly larger scale, depicts the group of Christ, John, Peter and Judas at the dramatic moment recounted in the Gospel of St. John (13: 21–26): "When Jesus had thus said, he was troubled in spirit, and testified, and said, 'Verily, verily, I say unto you, that one of you shall betray me'. Then the disciples looked one on another, doubting of whom he spake. Now there was leaning on Jesus' bosom one of his disciples, whom Jesus loved. Simon Peter therefore beckoned to him, that he should ask who it would be of whom he spake. He then lying on Jesus' breast said unto him, 'Lord, who is it?' Jesus answered, 'He it is, to whom I shall give a sop, when I have dipped it'. And when he had dipped the sop, he gave it to Judas Iscariot, the son of Simon".
The moment that Leonardo initially chose to portray, therefore, had already been artists' traditional choice for centuries: Christ's handing

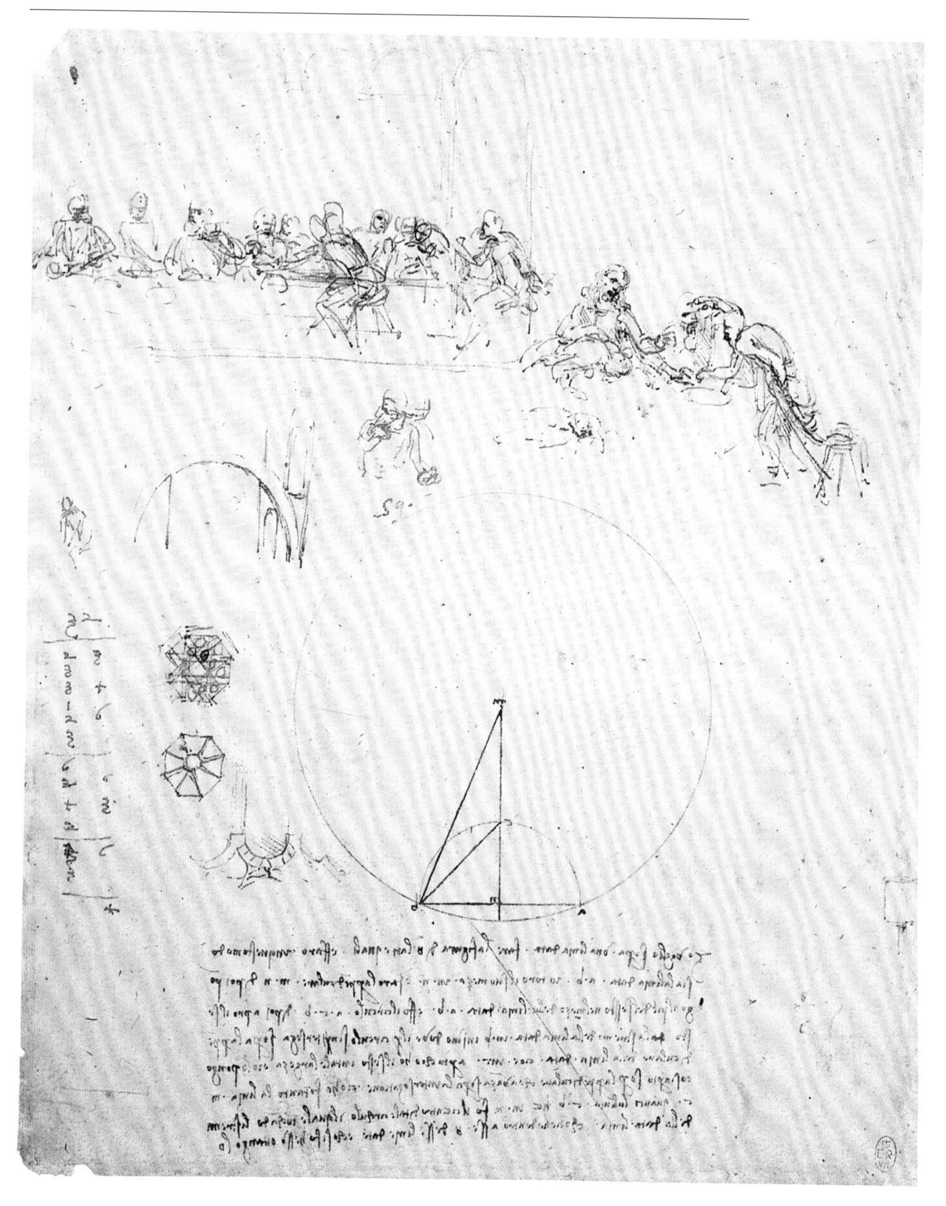

Leonardo da Vinci,
Four studies for the Last Supper, circa 1490–92
Pen and ink on paper,
266 x 214 mm
Windsor Castle, Royal Library (inv. RL 12542),
H.M. Queen Elizabeth II.

of the sop of bread to Judas is the sign that Judas is the traitor. As Jack Wasserman has observed, the earliest portrayals of this episode found in the Gospel of St. John include a relief in the cathedral of Volterra, another twelfth-century relief in San Giovanni Fuoricivitas in Pistoia, and a fresco dated to the same century in the abbey of Viboldone, just outside Milan (in the Gospel according to St. Luke, by contrast, it is the traitor's hands that give him away, as they clasp Christ's, but this scene has apparently never been painted)[2].
In the extraordinary detail of Christ's left arm, however, lies the most distinctive feature of Leonardo's drawing. The arm is sketched in two positions simultaneously: in the first it is outstretched, in the act of taking or handing the bread; in the other it is withdrawn, either pointing or reaching towards the plate. The resulting sequence is practically photographic, and lends the scene a vitality and motion only compounded by the astonished reaction of St. Peter, who stares at Judas with a stern, questioning look, his hand slapped to his forehead. The contrast with Christ's expression couldn't be more pronounced: Christ appears compassionate and resigned, despite his deep dismay. It is really quite remarkable how Leonardo could concentrate such a great variety of attitudes, gestures, expressions and meaning in a few square centimetres of paper, by means of a few pen strokes. His virtuosity makes us regret all the more that so much has vanished of the great mural, where surely the subtle variations, correspondences and colour resonances between one figure and another must have been much more numerous. It is their loss that makes the Windsor sheet all the more important, and doubtless the most significant of the studies for the painting to have survived[3].
Before we turn to Leonardo's masterpiece itself, there are still a number of observations to be made. Besides other figure drawings connected with

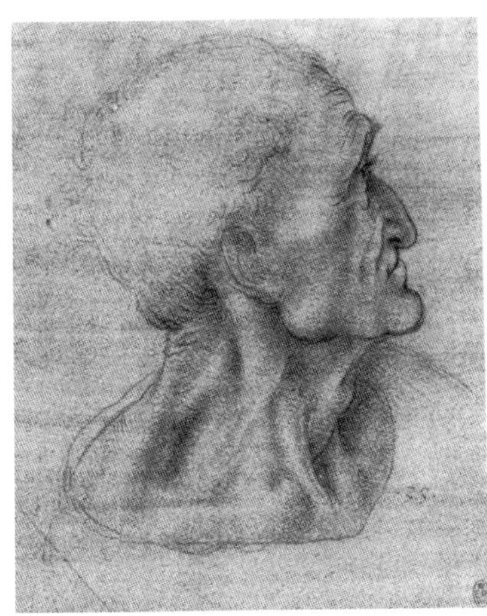

Leonardo da Vinci, *Study for Judas Iscariot*, Windsor Castle, Royal Library (inv. RL 12547), H.M. Queen Elizabeth II.

Study for the head of Philip, circa 1493–94
Black chalk on paper, 188 x 147 mm
Windsor Castle, Royal Library (inv. RL 12551), H.M. Queen Elizabeth II.

Leonardo da Vinci, *Head of male figure in profile facing right, circa* 1496–97
Red chalk on paper, 190 x 146 mm
Windsor Castle, Royal Library (inv. RL 12548), H.M. Queen Elizabeth II.

Study for the head of Saint James the Greater with four architectural drawings, circa 1492–94
Red chalk, pen and ink, 251 x 171 mm
Windsor Castle, Royal Library (inv. RL 12552), H.M. Queen Elizabeth II.

the *The Last Supper*, the sheet discussed here, Windsor 12542, both on the *recto* and the *verso,* contains several studies relating to architecture, geometry and mechanics. These drawings serve to confirm the dating of the sheet to around 1492–94, and are significant because they link the studies for *The Last Supper*, and the painting itself, to a particular phase of Leonardo's career, marked by an especially wide range of interests and investigations. The decade running from 1490 to 1499, in fact, was one of the busiest and most stimulating for the artist. Besides his painting commissions, in this period Leonardo also elaborated on his observations and compiled notes which he hoped to use as the basis for a consistent, organic treatise on painting in general, while also devoting himself to the study of motion and mechanical phenomena in particular. His studies of mechanics, ballistics, the repercussion of movements, visual rays and sound, as well as anatomy understood as a mechanical system applied to the human body, are already reflected in the Windsor drawing 12542r and all come to bear on *The Last Supper.*

In the painting, however, the moment of the Passion of Christ which Leonardo chooses to depict is not, as we have remarked earlier, the one to be found in the preparatory studies of the Windsor sheet. Although no existing documentation testifies to Leonardo's shift in subject matter, he has clearly chosen to portray the charged moments immediately preceding the identification of Judas, when Christ makes the dramatic statement: "One of you shall betray me". The apostles' highly emotional reaction is one of astonishment. Peter turns to John and motions for him to question Jesus, as he does in the verses from St. John's Gospel quoted above (in fact, John is not resting his head on Jesus' chest, as the traditional representations of the Last Supper dictate, but is sitting back in response to Peter's request for him to ask Christ for an explanation). It could be said that Christ's words, "One of you shall betray me", strike the apostles like the sound waves Leonardo studied, rebounding from one figure to another and in the process fashioning their very gestures, attitudes and movements. The artist has achieved

44

the remarkable feat of perfectly translating the diagram of a law of acoustics, optics and dynamics[4] into painting.
That the varying reactions of the apostles correspond to the different ways a light ray is reflected and rebounds, according to the type of surface refracting it, is confirmed by certain observations of Leonardo's in two passages from a manuscript exclusively devoted to problems of light and shade, the Institut de France Ms. C, f. 16r, dating from around 1490. This is how Leonardo compares the diffusion of sound and visual rays: "On reflected movements: I desire to define why bodily and spiritual movements, after striking the object, rebound at equal angles. On bodily movements: I say the re-echoing voice is reflected by striking the ear, as objects striking mirrors are reflected to the eye. And just as the image falls from the thing to the mirror and from the mirror to the eye at an equal angle, so the voice, when it first strikes the ear, will fall and rebound at equal angles in the cavity".
Elsewhere, in manuscripts almost entirely devoted to the problems inherent in painting, Leonardo compares the propagation of sound to that of visual rays, and likens these effects to the expanding circles of waves

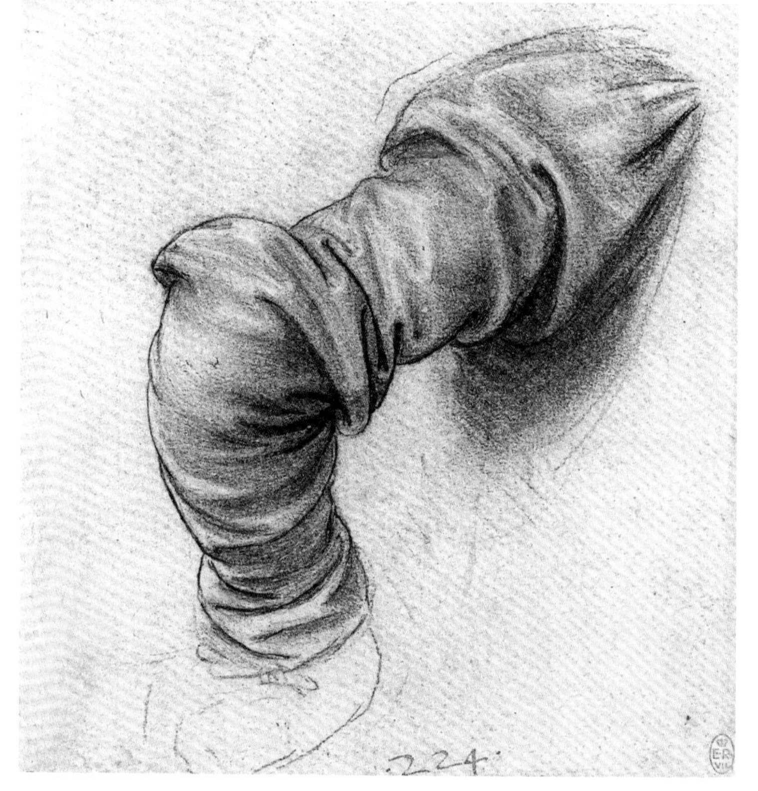

Leonardo da Vinci, *Study for the right arm of Peter, circa* 1493–94
Black chalk heightened with white lead and partially retouched with pen and sepia ink on paper, 166 x 154 mm
Windsor Castle, Royal Library (inv. RL 12546), H.M. Queen Elizabeth II.

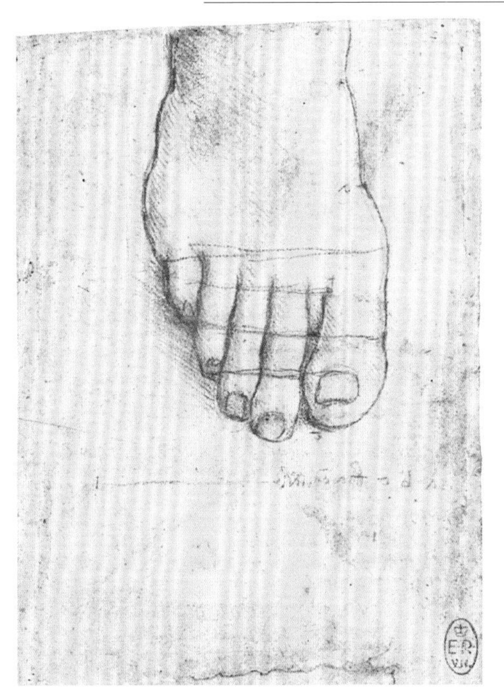

Leonardo da Vinci, *Study for the right foot of Christ, circa* 1493–94
Red chalk on paper, 99 x 70 mm
Windsor Castle, Royal Library (inv. RL 12635 *recto*), H.M. Queen Elizabeth II.

around a point struck on a watery surface. His observations appear, for example, in sheets 9v and 19v of the Paris Ms. A, 1490–92 circa, as well as in Ms. H, sheet 67 r[5] and in an older sheet, dating from around 1490, of the *Codex Atlanticus,* 10411r (ex f. 373r-b), which sets out the following conclusions: "The stone, where it strikes the surface of the water, causes circles around it which spread until they are lost; and in the same way the air, struck by a voice or a noise, also has a circular motion, so that he who is nearest hears it best and he who is most distant cannot hear it". The attitudes of the disciples around Christ seem to mirror this phenomenon.

Consequently, in approaching *The Last Supper*, we cannot overlook Leonardo's related studies in optics, mechanics and dynamics, which absorbed the artist in the years immediately preceding his commission for *The Last Supper* and during the years he was creating his masterpiece. Despite the perspectival plan which is almost too obvious (and so apparently simple that for this very reason it could well conceal another key to the interpretation of the work), another design suggests itself. That circular form which Leonardo always loved, considering it life-giving and a symbol of harmony, seems to dominate the composition; indeed, critics have often remarked on the grouping of the figures in threes, as if governed by a force which expands from the exact centre of the composition – Christ – outwards. That force then rebounds towards the centre from which it propagated just like a refracted wave – represented by the group of three apostles on Christ's immediate left, with James and Thomas leaning in his direction. However, this is hardly the only link between the multiple figures and movements.

The way the apostles are arranged around Christ seems to reflect a broader, more general scheme, which takes the form of a vast semicircle, similar to an apse. The greater visual weight of the figures at either end of the table, along with the receding of the intervening figures into deeper planes, serve to convey this impression. James the Greater's outspread arms appear to take the measure of the depth of this spacious niche – in an architectural design it would be a sort of *lunula* – and the draped table is placed exactly in the centre of the space. The very length of the

LV
BE
F
DVS

SF
DVX
AN

Bartholomew
James
the Lesser
Andrew
Simon
Peter
Judas
Iscariot
John

Jesus
Christ
Thomas
James
the Greater
Philip
Matthew
Judas
Thaddaeus
Simon
the Zealot

Leonardo da Vinci, *The Last Supper* The face of Christ (detail).

Following pages The groups of the apostles (details).

table, in turn, seems to generate the optical illusion of the table's being higher towards the centre; the figure of Christ is thus brought forward, which balances the effect of his drawing back from the table. As a result, around the central figure of Christ the disciples appear to be arranged like the spokes of a wheel, although in the axes composed of the figures there are variations that depart from the general circular design.

And subtler variations still may be discerned in the inclination of the figures' heads, much more so than in the expressive gestures of their hands, in which rhetorical devices may be at work. We see only two in exact profile, Bartholomew and Matthew, perpendicular to the table at opposite ends; Simon's head is in *profil perdu,* seemingly turning inside the space, while the others are either shown in three-quarter view or are tilted with respect to the painting's frontal plane, in variations that escape an orthogonal orientation. Even the second head from the left, apparently in profile, should in reality be slightly turned towards the foreground, as the Royal Academy version of the work (one of the earliest and most faithful copies) shows quite clearly. Christ's head is slightly smaller than the others (about 33 cm high), so as to define the vanishing point of the perspective and mark the real spatial depth from the plane constituted by the table. By contrast, the apostles' heads (including those on either end, Bartholomew and Simon, although they appear larger) are all the same height (36–37 cm approximately). However attenuated by the foreshortening of those placed obliquely to the plane of the painting itself, this overall uniformity in the size of the figures' heads is unsettling. They almost seem to be breaking through towards the frontal plane of the table; Thomas's head, for example, being drawn back, should therefore appear smaller, yet it is larger than Christ's.

This said, undoubtedly it was part of Leonardo's design to offer a very ample compendium of the *moti dell'anima,* the "motions of the soul", that is, reflected in the variety of attitudes and human expressions (indeed, his many drawings of caricatural and even "'grotesque" heads, in which he exploits his physiognomical studies to the hilt, may well all derive from his studies for the apostles' facial expressions). It would be hard to imagine another "test", or words other than those pronounced by Christ, that could have illustrated Leonardo's artistic and aesthetic theories so well. These ideas found expression in the memorandum of the *Forster Codex* II, ff. 62v-63r[6], coeval with *The Last Supper*, and in various notes for the *Treatise on Painting.* There we read, for example: "The movements of men vary with the variety of accidents running through their minds: and each accident in itself moves these men to a greater or lesser degree according to their greater force and age; because the same occurrence will cause a different movement in a young man

Leonardo da Vinci, *The Last Supper* From the left, the figures of James the Lesser and Andrew (detail).

than in an old one". We may note that the terminology the artist uses (movements, accidents, greater force, etc.) and the mental process he implies are the same Leonardo applied to the study of the causes of "accidental" or induced movement in mechanics and dynamics.

If we assume that this complex chain of "motions of the soul" and emotional reactions, as reflected in attitudes, gestures, and facial expressions, is the definitive version of the programmatic manifesto that Leonardo intended to leave to posterity (perfectly rendering the visualization of a passage in the Gospels), then the spatial context – the imaginary refectory in which Jesus and the apostles are sitting, with what first seems to be its rectangular form – appears to be no more than a container. The space is conceived not so much to give the illusion of continuity to the real refectory (although, considering the pale tones revealed by the restoration, along with the room's original lighting, that effect must have originally been far more obvious than today)[7], but to escalate the drama and focus the scene on Christ, the main actor in the story we see unfolding. Christ is the source of all the "movement", as Leonardo understands it. Indeed, his "motion is born of force" is an obvious allusion to Christ's spiritual force, if we bear in mind the artist's own definition of force as a "spiritual virtue", which, as Martin Kemp has recently observed, clearly foreshadows his later theories in which he refers to God, the "Prime Mover"[8], Christ's word, the Word of God, breathes life into the scene portrayed, it gives life and movement to the whole universe.

In light of the above, the problem of the perspectival construction of the *The Last Supper* may appear almost marginal. And even after all the incised lines brought to light in the upper part of the composition[9] have been fully studied, this is a problem that may never be solved, considering that Leonardo's own handling of the matter was deliberately ambiguous. The few solid reference points which would have allowed us to reconstruct the perspectival scheme seem to have been carefully hidden by the artist (in fact, the two painted walls project well beyond the frontal plane of the picture) and the room has been given an accelerated perspective; Leonardo was questioning the static perspective that epitomised the Florentine tradition at the time[10]. The result is not the perspectival image of a rectangular room, but the contracted image of a trapezoidal container. Once again, Leonardo's approach to perspective is not an isolated problem. It cannot be considered separately from the artist's theories concerning the "motions of the mind", the illustration of which was Leonardo's chief aim. Indeed, the architectonic space he depicted provided the artist with an opportunity to test other hypotheses, verify his theories on light and shadow, and exemplify them in a form which perfectly reflects the notes and diagrams found in the Paris Ms. C.

Leonardo used the painted room behind the apostles as a testing ground, to experiment with a highly complicated lighting situation. From the back come three different sources of illumination that mingle like three light beams shining into an optical box through different openings. And a stronger light comes from the left, one that Leonardo has roughly coincide with the real light coming through the windows on the left side of the refectory. Lastly, there is the light coming from the refectory itself, practically at right angles to the picture plane. In the painted room, the wall on the left is almost completely in shadow, but toward the vanishing point that shadow is dissipated by the light coming through the windows. By contrast, the right wall is almost completely illuminated except for a portion at the end (a vertical band of shade next to the last tapestry, a nuance which, unfortunately, has been almost completely lost in the original, but is clearly visible in a number of copies and in the Dutertre water-colour as well), with a shadow effect induced by the portion of the back wall that is next to the first window on the right; a shadow illuminated by the light source coinciding with that of the real windows. The exquisite drawings of the Paris Ms C reveal that this differentiated lighting is the result of dozens and dozen of studies Leonardo made of shadows themselves, "percussed and repercussed;" moreover, a passage in f. 14v seems to anticipate the "optical experiment" of which *The Last Supper* is the demonstration: "Repercussed shadow is that which is surrounded by lighted wall".

Leonardo da Vinci, *The Last Supper* From the left, the figures of Judas Iscariot, Peter and John (details).

Furthermore, what Leonardo has depicted in *The Last Supper* and his studies of the same period are so interrelated that another explanation of the painting simply fails to convince – particularly if it is taken to be the sole key to unlocking the painting's meaning –: the hypothesis that the *Supper* and the gestures of Christ and the apostles it portrays should be interpreted as symbolizing the institution of the Eucharist. This event, which precedes the revelation of Christ's imminent betrayal, would certainly not trigger such an emotional, dramatic reaction as we observe here in the apostles' movements and facial expressions. St. Mark (14, 22–25) says that: "And as they did eat,

Jesus took bread, and blessed, and brake it, and gave to them, and said: 'Take, eat: this is my body.' And he took the cup, and when he had given thanks, he gave it to them and they all drank of it. And he said unto them, 'This is my blood...'"
In the painting, however, there is no eating or drinking going on, much less blessing being bestowed, and Christ is simply not making the gestures described by St. Mark. Finally, not even Simon's attitude, on the far right, is any proof that he is in the act of receiving the bread and the wine, another post-restoration claim[11]. Simon's supposedly "ritual" gesture is none other than that we make when we hold out our hands when we don't understand, or question ourselves without finding an answer ("the other with hands outspread shows their palms... and his mouth expresses amazement" – this description fits the third apostle from the right, Andrew, but it also clearly shows that Simon's gestures are a reaction of astonishment at Christ's words).
Although Heydenreich also acknowledges that there may be an allusion to the institution of the Eucharist in the painting, he considers it as no more than a secondary meaning, and only after greatly insisting on the fact that the episode in Leonardo's *Last Supper* refers to the moment immediately prior to the announcement of the coming betrayal[12]. Reservations about Steinberg's hypothesis had previously been expressed by Anna Maria Brizio as well[13].
On the other hand, it is also inconceivable that the scene represents an image blocked like a freeze frame at one moment which carries a single meaning; after all, the painting is loaded with references and symbolic allusions, of which the institution of the Eucharist is only one. Certainly, a wall painting in a refectory could hardly fail to portray the eminently suitable, and traditional, theme of the *Last Supper*; Leonardo, however, enhanced his subject with the results of more than a decade of studies and experiments, but also crucial references and allusions connected with the Passion of Christ. The offer of self-sacrifice, to name one, in the ritual of the bread and wine, recalls the *Crucifixion* painted on the opposite wall of the refectory by Montorfano, and even the way Christ is seated alludes directly to the Crucifixion, with his arms outspread and his feet (once visible, before the door was opened in the wall below) slightly crossed – as shown in a drawing at Windsor. At the same time, once the Passion cycle is complete, the bread the friars of the Grazie eat and the wine they imbibe while seated at their meal become their spiritual nourishment as well. There may well be, then, symbolic meanings in the garlands of fruit and leaves that hang above the scene and fill the lunettes, which are placed high up between Leonardo's composition and the real space of the refectory itself, skilfully concealing the point where the

Leonardo da Vinci,
The Last Supper
From the left, the figures of Thomas, James the Greater and Philip (detail).

Leonardo da Vinci, *The Last Supper* The figure of Matthew (left) and Philip (above, details).

vaulted ceiling, once decorated with gold stars on a blue background, meets the painting of *The Last Supper*, where it certainly must have contrasted with the coffered ceiling the artist chose for his mural. The central lunette, with its inscription to Ludovico Sforza and Beatrice d'Este, dukes of Milan[14], features a garland enclosing a coat of arms in a chequered pattern, in contrasting colours. In a show of Leonardo's taste and particular sensibility, the Sforza snakes are painted a bright blue on a dark background, the latter made of fine silver leaf. As a final touch, the ribbons and coats of arms of all the lunettes were surely gilded, to heighten the impression of real shields hanging on the walls (just as on the opposite wall, the warriors' helmets are in relief, Montorfano's way of simulating metal armour in his painting). *Trompe l'œil* was employed for the garlands as well, particularly the one in the centre, and their use doubtless reflected the tradition of adorning the façades of churches and palaces with real wreaths of leaves (as is the case with the façade of Saint Mark's in Venice at Easter, for instance, even now). The custom of decorating palaces with festoons of this sort was strong in Milan, as well; as Barbara Fabjan has pointed out, on the occasion of Gian Galeazzo's betrothal to Isabella of Aragon in 1489, the walls of the Castle were hung with "swags of ivy and laurel made in the antique style", and the streets were festooned with "swags of greenery, ornamented with juniper, laurel and ivy", complete with the ducal insignia.

In fact, the recent restoration has brought to light the original outline of the shield-shaped coat of arms, which took the form of a bucrane, the very motif found in a drawing at Windsor Royal Library, no. 12282a-r; in a study for a Sforza emblem contained in the Paris Manuscript H; and also in a tondo adorning the outside of the apse of Santa Maria delle Grazie, which also features a "ducal motif"[15].

The left-hand lunette bears an epigraph that refers to the Sforzas' eldest son, Massimiliano, in his capacity as earl of Angera and Pavia[16], while the epigraph in the lunette on the right almost certainly celebrated Ludovico and Beatrice's second son, Francesco II, born in 1495, as Duke of Bari, although his name does not appear[17].

In several points leaves and fruits appear to have been repainted, which is confirmed by a fascinating series of ultraviolet and infrared photographs taken in the course of the restoration, published in 1986. The garlands do show the hand of Leonardo, particularly in the design of the beautiful winding ribbons, several lanceolate leaves found in the left lunette, the bright blue snakes remarked on above, and the general composition. They appear to have been painted, however, with heavy brush strokes, the paint too caked and the colour dull in places, despite the exceptionally good state of preservation of the leaves and several groups of fruit. That said, laboratory examinations suggest the same technique of execution for both the garlands above and *The Last Supper* below, the only difference being that the artist or artists painted the garlands (using tempera with an oily binding, it would appear) directly on a base coat of *intonaco*, without the white lead ground used for the *Supper.*

Leonardo da Vinci, *The Last Supper* From the left, the figures of Judas Thaddaeus and Simon the Zealot (detail).

We owe the exceptional state of preservation of the lunette paintings to the fact that they were brought to light only in 1854, emerging from under four coats of plaster. Ottino Della Chiesa believes that the lunettes were subjected to a "ruinous washing"[18], perhaps in the eighteenth century, making it feasible that both the repainting and the subsequent whitewashing were done more recently. However, the decorations seem to date to a much earlier period; if this is true, one could make the case that they were painted over immediately after the fall of Ludovico il Moro, that is, after 1499, the motive being what amounted to a *damnatio memoriae* that would remove the Sforza names and replace them, in all likelihood, with those of the King of France. It is also within the realm of possibility to suggest that upon Leonardo's return to Milan in 1506, he or one of his apprentices retouched the leafy decorations (certain group-

Leonardo da Vinci, *The Last Supper* From the left, the figures of Bartholomew and Matthew, Judas Thaddaeus and Simon the Zealot at either end of the painting (details).

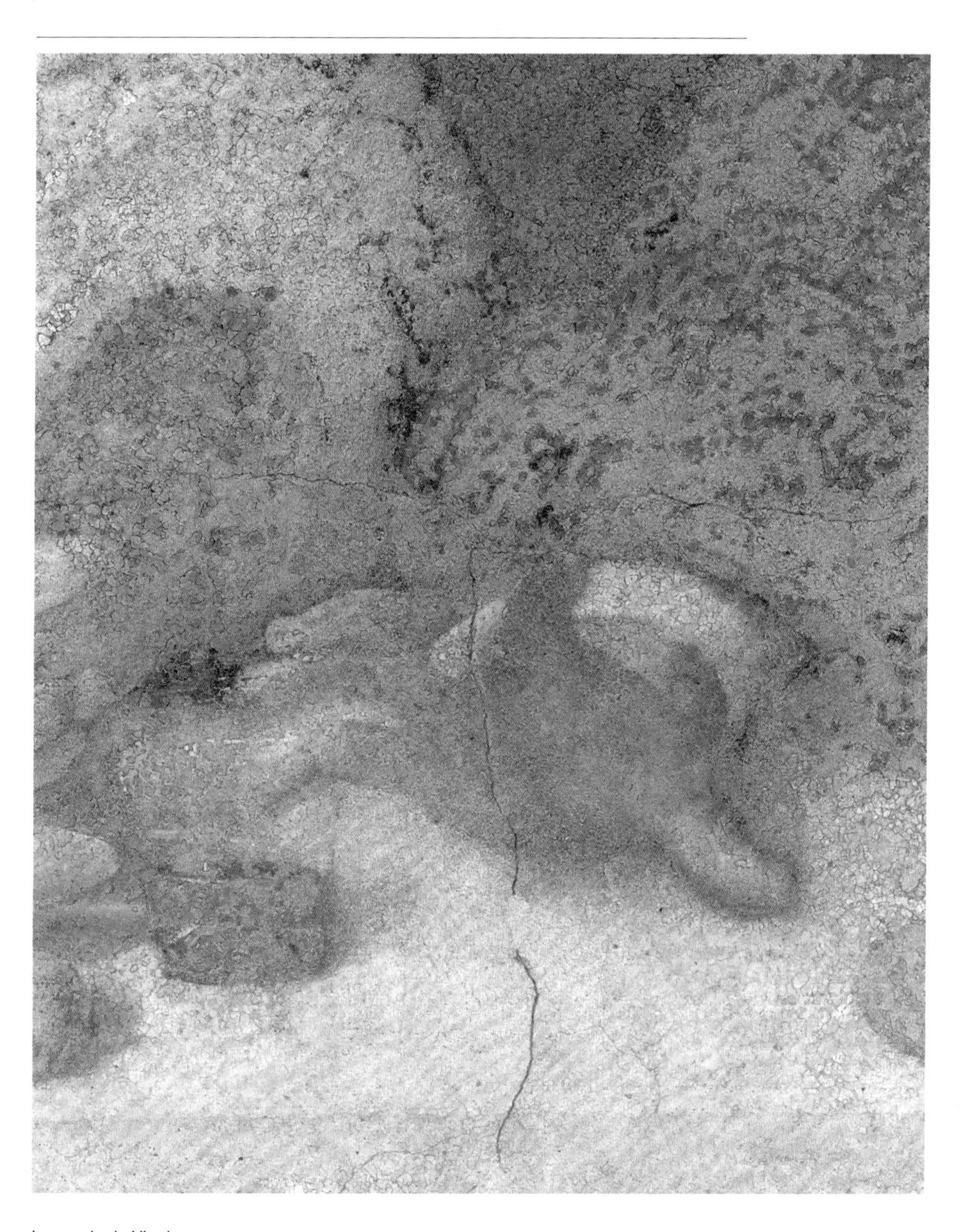

Leonardo da Vinci,
The Last Supper
The right hand
and the left hand
of Christ (details).

Leonardo da Vinci,
The Last Supper
Right and opposite, further details of hands: the left hands of Judas Iscariot, James the Lesser and Andrew, and the right hand of Judas with the pieces of silver (details).

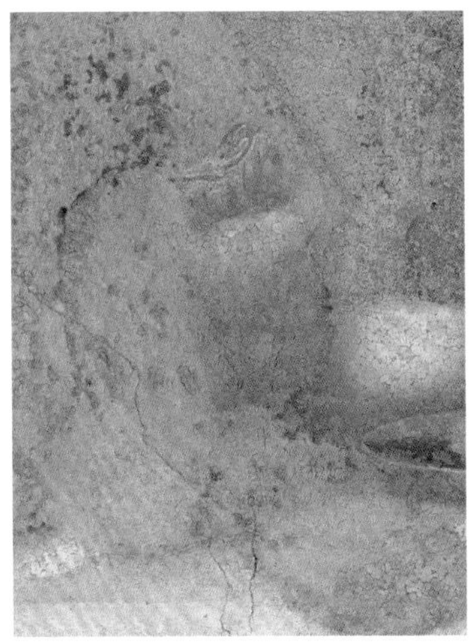

ings of leaves, in fact, are stylistically akin to the vegetation adorning the second version of the *Virgin of the Rocks*), restoring the parts that had flaked off or been damaged. We can only guess that the three lunettes were then covered over once more, since the first mention of the existing decorations is made by Giuseppe Mazza, as late as 1770[19]. There was a long and glorious tradition of motifs of swags and garlands in northern Italian painting; we need look no further than Mantegna's decorations for the *Camera degli Sposi* in Mantua, or Carlo Crivelli's paintings, among them the *Madonna della Candeletta* in the Brera Art Gallery; there is nothing surprising, therefore, about Leonardo's choice of this motif. Besides, the artist's fascination with vegetation is borne out by any number of extremely perceptive botanical drawings which reveal his extraordinary sensibility in rendering plants on canvas. Moreover, the first two lunettes in the long walls of the refectory would also seem to have been decorated by Leonardo. Unfortunately, only the brush drawing in the first lunette on the west wall has come down to us (the one on the east side was obliterated, together with the whole east wall itself, in the 1943 bombing). After this drawing was cleaned, Carlo Bertelli confirmed it to be an autograph work[20].

It is almost certain that Leonardo started working on the preparatory studies for *The Last Supper* in the first half of the final decade of the fifteenth century. The enlargement of the refectory of Santa Maria delle Grazie and its decoration were part of a broader programme designed to celebrate the Sforza dynasty and Ludovico il Moro in particular. The new chancel of the church, built to Bramante's design beginning in 1492, was overwhelmingly the most important and far-reaching project to be executed: it was intended to hold the tombs of Ludovico and his wife, sculpted by Cristoforo Solari, now preserved in the Certosa of Pavia. The monumental complex had been redesigned as a sort of mausoleum, therefore, its theological and religious significance underlying its symbolic and celebrative function[21]. In contributing to this ambitious programme, Bramante and Leonardo are linked by the consonance between the architectural ideals of the former and the new, monumental scale adopted by the latter for his figures in *The Last Supper*, in which an architectural ideal may be discerned as well, possibly of Bramantesque inspiration (compare Leonardo's figure of Simon with those of the *Men at Arms* in the Casa Panigarola, now at Brera). The illusionistic quality of Leonardo's painted architecture finds an echo in Bramante's *trompe l'œil* choir in the church of San Satiro, although the overt scenographic intent of the latter is ultimately secondary in Leonardo's mural, as we said. Lastly, in 1495 Donato Montorfano had completed his *Crucifixion* on the wall opposite *The Last Supper*, although this commission seems to have arrived from the Dominican friars of Santa Maria delle Grazie. As a letter to Marchesino Stanga reveals, Ludovico il Moro himself took an active interest in Leonardo's *Supper*, asking Stanga to solicit the artist "so that he may finish the work begun in the refectory of the Grazie and subsequently attend to another wall of this refectory". The letter, dated 29 June 1497[22], furnishes evidence that Leonardo was possibly given a commission to decorate the wall which had been entrusted to Montorfano and completed just two years earlier; it also provides a crucial parameter for dating the conclusive phase of Leonardo's work. We know that *The Last Supper* was finished in the following year, 1498, as Luca Pacioli reports in the well-known passage from his *De divina proportione*[23] quoted above. To arrive at a date for the start of the project, then, we must consider the length of time required to work out the scheme and make preliminary studies (of which nothing has come down to us if not the early ones shown in the Windsor sheet, already discussed in depth, and the drawings of the apostles' heads, which belong, however, to the final stage of preparation). If the painting technique chosen by Leonardo (not *buon fresco*, the execution of

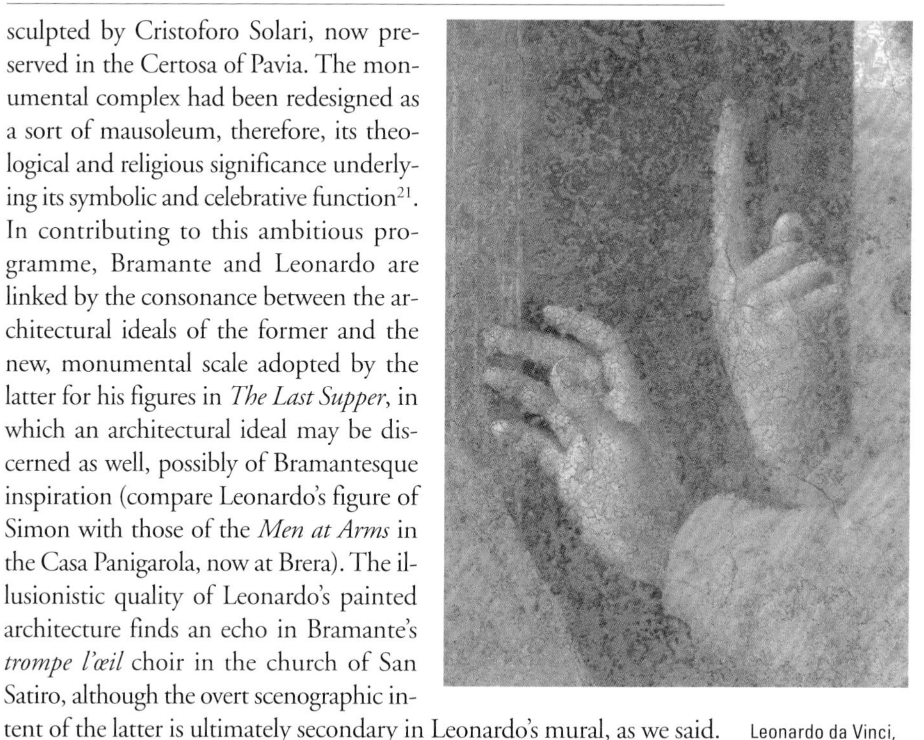

Leonardo da Vinci, *The Last Supper*
Above and opposite, the hands of James the Greater, Thomas and Philip (details).

Leonardo da Vinci,
The Last Supper
Above, the hands of Simon
the Zealot; opposite,
the right hand of Peter
holding a knife (details).

Leonardo da Vinci, *The Last Supper*. Details of the laid table: water jug, glass, plate with reflections (details).

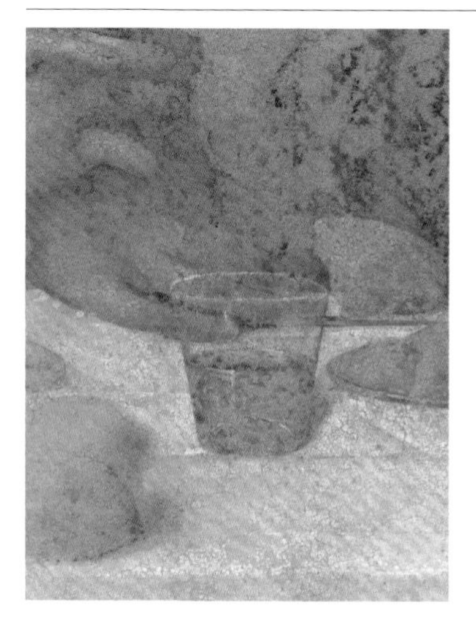

which was almost immediate, but a technique which would allow him to make subtle changes and add further touches later, as Matteo Bandello recounts in his famous novella)[24] is factored into the equation, the start of Leonardo's work in the refectory needs to be backdated by at least four or five years, to around 1494, if not earlier[25].
This chronology seems to be borne out by the scientific observations and notes on the theory of painting quoted above, all of which are contained in manuscripts datable between 1490 and 1494. Moreover, another element for dating *The Last Supper*, regularly overlooked, is a first-hand testimony by Bandello, who recalls often seeing Leonardo on his way to the Grazie to paint the *Supper*, and makes an important reference to the equestrian monument to Francesco Sforza: "I have also seen him, according to how the caprice or impulse took him, set out at midday, when the sun is in Leo, from the Corte Vecchia, where he was working on his marvellous clay horse, come straight to the Grazie and, climbing on the scaffolding, take the brush and give a few strokes to one of the figures, then immediately leave and go elsewhere".
For the chronology of our *Last Supper*, it would be very interesting if we could determine exactly how far along the project for the Sforza monument Leonardo was at the time Bandello wrote. We do know that Leonardo had returned to work on his studies for the horse in 1490 (after an initial start most likely in 1482–83); indeed, the Codex 8937 in the Biblioteca Nacional of Madrid, discovered in 1965, mentions the final studies for a second version, the completion of a clay model and, finally, the casting of the statue in 1493: "20th of December 1493... I finished casting the horse without the tail and on its side". If the horse was cast on that date, however, the clay model must have been ready

Leonardo da Vinci, *The Last Supper*. Details of the laid table: plates, slice of orange, glass (details).

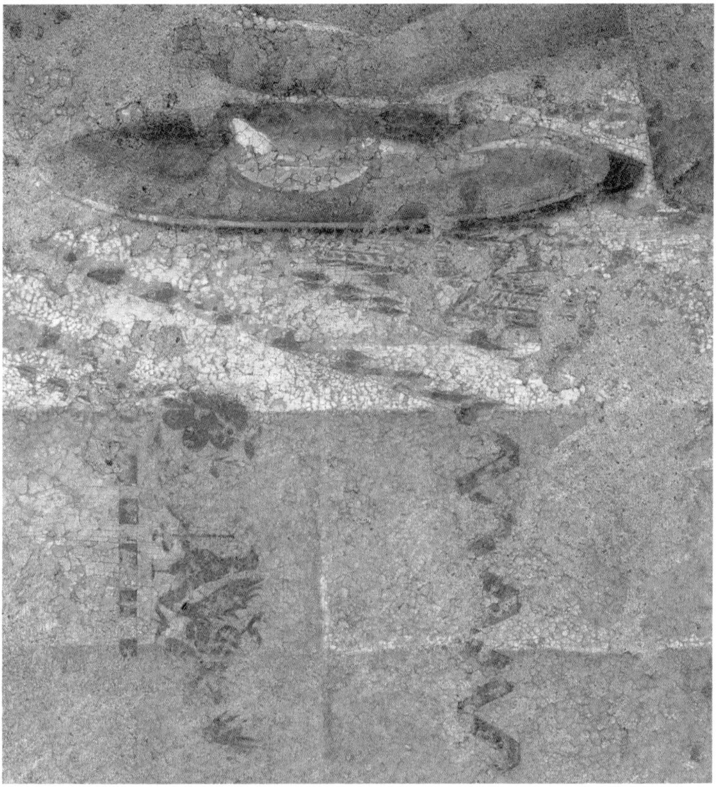

Leonardo da Vinci, *The Last Supper.* Details of the laid table: blue embroidery of the tablecloth (detail).

some time earlier, considering that Leonardo's revolutionary method for casting statues involved obtaining the wax model from the clay model one piece at a time[26]. It is important to note that, if Bandello is to be believed, Leonardo was working on the clay model for the Sforza monument and *The Last Supper* at the same time. Since after 1494–95 work on the "great horse" seems to have been interrupted ("I will say nothing of the horse because I know the times")[27] and Bandello's reference to "a few strokes" can only allude to Leonardo's working on the *Supper* at a very advanced stage, we can suppose that Bandello had a period closer to 1492–93 than 1494–95 in mind (a remark he makes before mentioning the clay model for the horse, about a visit by the Cardinal of Gurk that took place in 1497, is of no help in dating the description of Leonardo's routine that follows).

The painting had already begun to deteriorate only twenty years after its completion: visiting the *Supper* in 1517–18, Antonio de Beatis found it "very excellent, although it is beginning to be spoiled, due either to the dampness of the wall or to some other accident"[28]. Fifty years later, the state of the painting was surely even more deplorable, which only fuelled rumours, unfounded, that serious mistakes in the execution were the cause of the decay, something Vasari, born in Arezzo, couldn't resist repeating, spitefully remarking that the work "was so badly done that nothing can be seen any more but a faded smudge"[29]. Lomazzo tried to put things right and excuse the maestro by claiming that *imprimitura* was unsuitable for an oil painting. As early as 1587, with Armenini, who found it "half spoiled although most beautiful", we see the first glimmerings of a fashion for decaying masterpieces, in a foreshadowing of Romantic tastes. Subsequent appraisals, ranging from that of Scannelli (1642) to the accounts of Lattuada (1738), de Brosses (1738), Bartoli (1776) and Domenico Pino (1796), are intertwined with more critical examinations which addressed the results and questioned the methodology of the first recorded attempts at "restoration" by Michelangelo Bellotti in 1726 and Giuseppe Mazza in 1770 (although traces of even earlier interventions have been brought to light).

The first intervention met with both praise and criticism (the latter particularly on the part of Bianconi, 1787) because Bellotti repatched the work using tempera or gouache and covered the whole wall with a layer of oil (with the result of hiding the original painting under his restoration, which seems, at least, to have spared the figures of Judas, Peter, John and Christ). Mazza set out to remove Bellotti's additions with a scraper, filling in the blank areas with an oil mixture, especially on Bartholomew and, to a lesser extent, on James and Andrew[30].

Leonardo da Vinci, *The Last Supper*. Details of the laid table: the knotted corner of the tablecloth (detail).

After a thorough inspection of the painting by Andrea Appiani in 1802 established that the paint was flaking off due to the dampness of the wall, and also ruled out the feasibility of detaching the the mural altogether and moving it, in 1821 Stefano Barezzi made a fresh attempt – limited to the area of the tablecloth beneath the figures of Bartholomew and Christ – to determine whether or not a transfer was possible by means of consolidating the painting with glue and adding coloured, wax-based stuccoes. In 1853–55 the same Barezzi consolidated and cleaned the whole surface, (as mentioned earlier, it was Barezzi who removed the plaster that concealed the decorations in the lunettes).

Pinin Brambilla Barcilon published a 1985 study that included some remarkable photographs of these early restoration attempts: one can make out Bellotti's repainting of Thaddeus' eyes and decorations of the tablecloth, Mazza's retouching of Thomas' eyes, and Barezzi's incisions on the table as well as the flattening of the painting's surface in the places where he had tried to detach the painting, only to fill them in with a wax-based material[31]. With the coming of the twentieth century, restorations were finally conducted on the additional basis of physical analyses of the painting's environmental conditions and chemical components, which allowed for the mural to be consolidated, for what it was possible, and allowed Cavenaghi to establish, in 1908, that *The Last Supper* had been executed in tempera on two preparation layers. In 1924 Silvestri carried out a new cleaning and a new consolidation (and applied plaster to the edges of the painted base surface).

Yet every prior effort to save the painting seemed to have been in vain, in the wake of the bombing of 1943 and the consequent reconstruction of the refectory's east wall. In fact, the rebuilding of the wall and floor had raised so much dust and released so much condensed humidity that Wittgens found the painting blackened and obscured: "Instead of somewhat white, it appeared completely black... the surface of the *Cenacolo*, swollen with humidity, looked like a rubbery fabric and at the least touch not only the paint but also the underlying chalk priming came away..."[32]. Hence the then Superintendent, Ettore Modigliani, appointed Mauro Pellicioli to attempt a new consolidation of the mural surface, "to be done more radically than the previous work by Cavenaghi and Silvestri". In 1947 Pellicioli went about binding the flaking paint to the plaster by brushing on the surface de-waxed shellac dissolved in alcohol, and then injecting casein behind it. The operation was a success: the shellac restored the paint its cohesion, consistency and bright colours; now it was on to the next stage of reclaiming Leonardo's original work, a task which Pellicioli carried out in 1951–52 and 1954.

Wittgens was quick to point out that Pellicioli had concentrated his efforts on the areas where "the eighteenth century colours had hidden the brilliant treasure of Leonardo's own painting". In fact, while Pellicioli's prudent, conservative cleaning did reveal some extraordinary finds – the Assisi embroidery on the tablecloth, the blue of Judas' robe with its decoration in gold Cufic letters – it stopped short of removing all the additions of previous centuries. Pinin Brambilla remarks that "one notes a greater care, in fact, to remove the repainting on the flesh, while the reworking of the eyes and the dark outlines of the faces and hands remain, and he has not insisted on removing the stratifications deposited on the abrasions or in the gaps to avoid making the picture unintelligible"[33]. Consequently, on entire areas the repaintings were left intact, including the coffered ceiling, the walls hung with tapestries and the lower portion below the table.

Leonardo da Vinci, *The Last Supper*. Details of the background: the flowers in the tapestry (detail).

Leonardo da Vinci, *The Last Supper.* Details of the background: the flowers in the tapestry (details).

The restoration completed in 1999 could hardly have been put off any longer: the environmental conditions of the refectory and the wall holding Leonardo's painting had steadily deteriorated during the sixties and seventies, leading to the depositing of a thick layer of dust and smog on the mural, among other damage. In view of a new cleaning, preliminary examinations of the work were started in 1976 under the supervision of the Superintendent for Artistic and Historical Heritage in Milan, at that time directed by Franco Russoli. He was succeeded by Stella Matalon, Carlo Bertelli, Rosalba Tardito and Pietro Petraroia in that order (my own collaboration dates to 1992), who have always had the benefit of Pinin Brambilla Barcilon's expertise. Thanks to scientific progress and the evolution of technology, every conceivable kind of analysis and examination was performed: chemical, physical, environmental, static, structural, and climatic; along with a photographic documentation nothing short of exhaustive[34], all of this under the aegis of the Istituto Centrale per il Restauro. Concurrently a restoration methodology was designed and applied, with the aim of salvaging whatever was left by Leonardo's own hand, and remove the historic as well as more recent repaintings that had largely hidden it from our view up to the present day.
However, the totality of the mural's repainted portions has not been removed. For example, the coffered ceiling we see is in fact an eighteenth-century reworking (although on the right a small section of the original has been brought to light), and so are the tapestries, even if on the left, under the heavy coating of an eighteenth-century repainting, some bunches of flowers belonging to the original composition have been discovered. In addition, the head of Judas, in very poor

condition, has preserved in its eighteenth-century form, after the removal of recent layers of colour that has restored much of the original profile. Nevertheless, the guiding principle of this restoration was by no means a purely aesthetic one: the complex, highly delicate situation, a direct result of Leonardo's original choice of technique, was compounded over the centuries by repeated repaintings and the layers of grime, mould and all the different materials that have accumulated on the painting's face. The host of consequences includes cleavage, the flaking off of paint and plaster, and variable reactions to heat and humidity. The adherence to this restoration methodology is a courageous policy has allowed for the retrieval of pictorial fragments that enable us to view for the very first time Leonardo's "original" painting (albeit preserved in a fragmentary state and damaged by no less than nine previous restoration efforts), and his colours in particular[35]. On the extreme right, the figure of Simon has seen its volume and monumentality restored (with more of Bramante than Michelangelo in the latter), along with its iridescent lilac and white tones. Matthew has regained his noble profile and the wave of emotion pervading him, and his tunic is once again an intense, brilliant blue. There is sorrow, but not pathos, in Philip's expression; James the Greater's face is vividly sculpted in its three-quarter view, an exclamation of amazement frozen on his parted lips; yet his expression has none of the caricature of the related Windsor drawing.

After acquainting visitors with these fragments of painting – of the highest artistic quality, despite the fact that so few have survived, and glowing with a remarkable light that seems to regenerate even the surrounding areas where everything but the ground is lost – and turning a backward glance on the portions on the left where the original heads of Bartholomew, Andrew, Peter and John have re-emerged (after previous interventions had distorted, and enlarged, nearly all of them), we can now fully appreciate the meticulous work that has "unbridled" the painting, constrained and almost suffocated in the course of one restoration after another. The beautiful heads of Bartholomew and James the Lesser – which recall the busts of antiquity – can now vaunt their original design and no small part of their former beauty, a perfect counterpoint to that of Matthew.

[1] Cf. K. Clark, *The Drawings of Leonardo da Vinci in the Collection of Her Majesty the Queen at Windsor Castle*, second edition revised with the aid of C. Pedretti, London 1968–69. vol. I, pp. 99–100.
[2] Cf. J. Wasserman, "Reflections on the Last Supper of Leonardo da Vinci", in *Arte Lombarda*, 66, no. 3, 1983, pp. 19–20, figs. 6–8.
[3] Among the other preparatory studies, there are the following sheets from Windsor Royal Library: nos. 12551 and 12552 (the heads of Philip and James the Greater), 12546 (Peter's right arm), 12543 (John's hands) and 12635r (Christ's feet); doubts have been raised concerning the authenticity of sheets no. 12547 (Judas' head, which, however, apparently should be considered authentic), 12548 (either the head of Bartholomew or, according to Berenson, that of Matthew: the drawing is almost universally accepted to be an original; doubts about its authenticity have been raised by Carlo Pedretti), 12549 and 12550 (which are in fact copies of a drawing by Leonardo for the head of Simon), 12544 and 12545 (copies of drawings for the hands of Matthew and Thomas). For all these sheets, cf. K. Clark, *op. cit.* pp. 100–2 and 133, and for other related studies, see the catalogue by C. Pedretti, *Leonardo. Studi per il Cenacolo*, Milan 1983, *passim.* Of all the preparatory drawings for the *Last Supper*, I have not considered the sheet in the Accademia of Venice, which is suspected of being a counterfeit (cf. A.M. Brizio, "Lo studio degli Apostoli nella Cena dell'Accademia di Venezia", in *Raccolta Vinciana*, XVIII, 1959, p. 45 ff., and XX, 1964, p. 414) although later scholars have started to rehabilitate it (cf. C. Pedretti. *Leonardo da Vinci inedito. Tre saggi*, Florence 1968, pp. 56–60; in her 1966 catalogue of the Venice drawings, Luisa Cogliati Arano had agreed it was counterfeit, but is now wavering: cf. L. Cogliati Arano, *I disegni di Leonardo* e *della sua cerchia alla Galleria dell'Accademia*, Milan 1980, pp. 56–57). In all likelihood the drawing was begun by Leonardo, who wrote in the apostles' names himself, but was altered and completed by a Milanese artist far less talented than the *maestro*. An interesting comparison may be made with the famous drawing of the *Head of Christ* at the Brera Art Gallery, about which there is a renewed hypothesis that it is an original drawing by Leonardo that was subsequently altered by one or more artists (cf. P.C. Marani, in *Disegni lombardi del Cinque e Seicento della Pinacoteca di Brera e dell'Arcivescovado*, Florence 1986, pp. 27–31).
[4] Cf. P.C. Marani, "Leonardo dalla scienza all'arte – Un cambiamento di stile, gli antefatti, una cronologia", in *Fra Rinascimento, manierismo e realtà – Scritti di storia dell'arte in memoria di Anna Maria Brizio*, Florence 1984, p. 44.
[5] Published by A.M. Brizio, *Scritti scelti di Leonardo da Vinci*, Turin 1952 (1966 edition, pp. 252–54).
[6] Cf. J.P. Richter, *The Literary Works of Leonardo da Vinci*, Oxford 1883 (1970 edition, paragraphs 665 and 666).
[7] The theory that the stationary point Leonardo chose for the perspectival construction of the *Last Supper* coincides with that of the real viewer was discarded in the wake of the discovery that, in actual fact, the perspectival point of view is located about four metres above the origi-

Leonardo da Vinci, *The Last Supper.* Details of the background: the ceiling and wall (detail).

Leonardo da Vinci, *The Last Supper.* Details of the background: the bell tower in the countryside behind Christ (detail).

nal level of the room's floor. For other studies on the perspective of the *Cenacolo*, see the bibliographical note added to the new edition of A.M. Brizio, *Leonardo da Vinci – Il Cenacolo,* Florence 1983.
[8] M. Kemp, *Leonardo da Vinci – The Marvellous Works of Nature and Man*, London 1981, pp. 261–329.
[9] Mentioned by Carlo Bertelli in the first accounts of the restoration then in progress: cf. note 35.
[10] On Leonardo's rediscovery of mediaeval optics see the fundamental report by A.M. Brizio, *Razzi incidenti e razzi refressi (III lettura vinciana)*, Florence 1963.
[11] C. Bertelli, in L.H. Heydenreich, *Invito a Leonardo – L'Ultima Cena*, Milan 1982, p. 8. The theory that Leonardo meant to portray the institution of the Eucharist dates back to von Einem and has later been relaunched by L. Steinberg. Others reject this view, including A. Ottino Della Chiesa (*L'opera completa di Leonardo pittore*, Milan 1967, p. 8), who seizes on a pertinent passage by Pacioli in his *De divina proportione*: "It is impossible to imagine the Apostles more attentively alive to the sound of the voice of the ineffable truth when it spoke: 'Unus vestrum me traditurus est'. With actions and gestures from one to another, with vivid and and pained amazement they seem to speak to each other, so nobly did our Leonardo arrange them with his graceful hand" (1498). Additional consideration should be given to the earliest engravings, attributed to Zoan Andrea or to the Master of the Sforza Book of Hours, where a label bears the words with which Christ announces his imminent betrayal (a reproduction of one of these engravings is found, for example, in L.H. Heydenreich, *op. cit.*, p. 103: others in C. Alberici, M. Chirico De Biasi, *Leonardo e l'incisione*, Milan 1984, pp. 59–61.
[12] L.H. Heydenreich, *op. cit.*, pp. 41–48.
[13] A.M. Brizio, "Il Cenacolo", in *Leonardo. La pittura*, Florence 1977, pp. 106–7.
[14] The inscription "LV[dovicus] MA[ria] BE[atrix] EST[ensis] SF[ortia] AN[glus] DVX [Mediolani]" now appears in white along the coat of arms and the garland, standing out against the red ground of the priming.
[15] Cf. C. Pedretti, *op cit.*, pp. 86–91.
[16] "MA[ria] M[a]X[imilianus] SF[ortia] AN[glus] CO[mes] P[a]P[iae]".
[17] "SF[ortia] AN[glus] DVX BARI". Francesco II was made Duke of Bari in 1497. This year is generally taken as the outer limit for dating the lunettes, which are traditionally thought to have been executed between 1495 (the birth of his second son) and 1497 (the bestowal of the title of Duke of Bari). The dating proposed for the lunettes does not, however, clash with what is said below about a possible antedating of the start of the work on *The Last Supper*.
[18] A. Ottino Della Chiesa, *op. cit.*, p. 99.
[19] Cf. B. Fabjan, "Il Cenacolo nuovamente restaurato", in *Leonardo – La pittura*, Florence 1985, p. 93, note l.
[20] C. Bertelli, *op. cit.*, pp. 12 and 145.
[21] See S. Lang's essay "Leonardo's Architectural Designs and the Sforza Mausoleum", in *Journal of the Warburg and Courtauld Institutes*, vol. XXXI, 1968, pp. 218–33. Also see M. Rossi. "Novità per

Leonardo da Vinci, *The Last Supper*. Details of the background: the nails holding the tapestry (above) and the cupboard behind Matthew (opposite, details).

Santa Maria delle Grazie di Milano". in *Arte Lombarda*, 66, 1983, pp. 35–70, and for other related articles, P.C. Marani, "Leonardo e le colonne 'ad tronchonos' – Tracce di un programma iconologico per Ludovico il Moro", in *Raccolta Vinciana*, XXI, 1982, pp. 103–20.

[22] Practically all of the existing literature on *The Last Supper* quotes this letter in its entirety: see in L. Beltrami, *Documenti* e *memorie riguardanti la vita e le opere di Leonardo da Vinci*, Milan 1919, pp. 48–49.

[23] Cf. above, note 12.

[24] M. Bandello, *Le novelle*, Bari 1910, vol. II, p. 283.

[25] The passage by Leonardo in the Paris Manuscript H, f. 64, dated 29 January 1494, examined by L.H. Heydenreich as well (*op. cit.*, p. 32, n. 3) in support of a proposed dating of Leonardo's commission to paint the *Cenacolo* to 1494, is not convincing, however. In fact, "il pian delle mura", "la sala" and "la ghirlanda" of which Leonardo speaks refer to the Castle of Milan, not to *The Last Supper*. The error was caught by Pedretti, *op. cit.*, p. 70, and independently by P.C. Marani, *L'architettura fortificata negli studi di Leonardo da Vinci, con il catalogo completo dei disegni*, Florence 1984, pp. 139–40.

[26] On the "Sforza horse", cf. M.V. Brugnoli, "Il monumento Sforza", in *Leonardo*, edited by L. Reti, Milan 1974, pp. 86–109.

[27] The mention is found in the draft of a letter to Ludovico il Moro which also mentions a commission "to paint the small rooms" in the Castle and which Brizio places earlier than a text in the Paris Manuscript H dated 1494. Cf. A.M. Brizio, *op. cit.*, 1952 (1966, pp. 639–40).

[28] L. Pastor, *Die Reise dess Cardinals Luigi d'Aragona*, Freiburg 1905.

[29] Vasari, *Le vite de' più eccellenti pittori scultori e architetti*, Florence 1568.

[30] For this and the following information, cf. B. Fabjan, *op. cit.*, p. 93 ff., note 1.

[31] P. Brambilla Barcilon, *Il Cenacolo di Leonardo in Santa Maria delle Grazie – Storia, condizioni, problemi*, Milan 1985, fig. 1, pp. 15–19.

[32] F. Wittgens, "Restauro del Cenacolo", in *Leonardo – Saggi* e *ricerche*, edited by the "Comitato Nazionale per le Onoranze a Leonardo da Vinci nel quinto centenario della nascita", Rome 1954, pp. 3–4.

[33] P. Brambilla Barcilon, *op. cit.*, p. 66.

[34] See, for example, the report by the Istituto Centrale del Restauro in Rome, dated 20 September 1977; the report by H. Travers Newton of 10 September 1977; the thermohygrometric tests performed by the Centro "Gino Bozza" of Milan in September 1979; the tests for the levels of air pollution in the room holding *The Last Supper* conducted by the Stazione Sperimentale per i Combustibili, Milan, on 18 October 1979, etc., all in Soprintendenza per i Beni Artistici e Storici di Milano, Archivio corrente, 13/31. See also M. Matteini, A. Moles, "A Preliminary Investigation of the Unusual Technique of Leonardo's Mural 'The Last Supper'", in *Studies in Conservation*, 24, 1979, pp. 125–33, and the analyses published in *Arte Lombarda*, 62, 1982. Cf. also H. Travers Newton, "Leonardo da Vinci as Mural Painters: Some Observations on His Materials and Working Methods", in *Arte Lombarda*, 66, 1983, pp. 71–88.

[35] See the reports on the first sensational discoveries: C. Bertelli, B. Fabjan, "Il Cenacolo di Leonardo", in *Brera – Notizie della Pinacoleca,* autumn-winter 1981–82, pp. 1–4; C. Bertelli, *op. cit.*, pp. 127–56; C. Bertelli, "Il Cenacolo vinciano", in *Santa Maria delle Grazie*, Milan 1983, pp. 188–95; D.A. Brown, *Leonardo's Last Supper: the Restoration*, Washington D.C. 1983; B. Fabjan, *op. cit.*, pp. 90–4. See also C. Bertelli, "Verso il vero Leonardo": in *Leonardo e Milano*, edited by G.A. Dell'Acqua, Milan 1982, pp. 83–8.

Bibliographical note

Further to the studies listed above, accounts of the restoration project as it proceeded chronologically, from top to bottom and right to left, have been provided by: C. Bertelli, B. Fabjan, "Il Cenacolo di Leonardo", in *Brera – Notizie della Pinacoleca,* autumn-winter 1981–82, pp. 1–3; C. Bertelli, "Verso il vero Leonardo": in *Leonardo e Milano*, edited by G.A. Dell'Acqua, Milan 1982, pp. 83–88; C. Bertelli, in L.H. Heydenreich, *Invito a Leonardo...* cit., 1983, pp. 127–56; Id., "Il Cenacolo vinciano", in *Santa Maria delle Grazie in Milan*, Milan 1983, pp. 188–95; D.A. Brown, *Leonardo's Last Supper. The restoration*, Washington D.C. 1983; P. Brambilla Barcilon, *Il Cenacolo di Leonardo…*, cit., 1984; B. Fabjan in *Leonardo. La pittura*, 1985, pp. 90–94; C. Bertelli. "Leonardo e l'Ultima Cena (c. 1595–97)", in *Tecnica* e *stile: esempi di pittura murale del Rinascimento italiano*, eds. E. Borsook and F. Superbi Gioffredi, The Harvard University Center for Italian Renaissance Studies at Villa I Tatti, Florence 1986, pp. 31–42; P. Brambilla Barcilon and P.C. Marani, "Le lunette di Leonardo nel Refettorio delle Grazie", in *Quaderni del Restauro*, 7, 1990; P.C. Marani, "Leonardo's Last Supper: Some Problems of Restoration and New Light on Leonardo's Art", in *Nine Lectures on Leonardo da Vinci*, eds. A. Bednarek and F. Ames Lewis, London 1990, pp. 45–52; id., "Le alterazioni dell'immagine dell'*Ultima Cena* di Leonardo dopo le più recenti analisi," in *Kermès. Arte e tecnica del restauro*, III, no. 7, 1990, pp. 64–67.

An initial photographic documentation of the right-hand section of the newly restored composition (including the figure of Christ) has been published in P.C. Marani, *Leonardo*, Milan 1994 (other editions: (Madrid 1995; Paris 1996). The analyses performed during the most recent restoration have finally established the medium adopted by Leonardo: tempera (perhaps mixed with oil) applied to two layers of base, the first a thicker layer of calcium carbonate, the second a thinner layer to which a white lead paint was applied. See H. Kuhn, "Bericht über die naturwissenschaftliche Untersuchungen der Malerei des Mailänder Abendmahls", in *Maltechnik*, IV, 1985, pp. 24–5l. The most significant analyses carried out on the Leonardo's painting, the physical and chemical findings, and the precautions taken for its conservation have been published in a study edited by G. Basile and M. Marabelli, *Leonardo. L'Ultima Cena. Indagini, ricerche, restauro,*, Rome-Florence 2007 (cf. the review by P.C. Marani, *Sul Cenacolo di*

Leonardo: trent'anni di studi e ricerche, in "La Ca' Granda", Fondazione Policlinico di Milano, Vol. XLVIII, nn. 3–4, 2008, pp. 27–28). The final report on the restoration and all new information to result are to be found in P.C. Marani and P. Brambilla Barcilon, *Leonardo. L'Ultima Cena*, Milan 1999. After its completion, much commentary and some doubts has been raised by the restoration that started with attempts to clean the work back in 1977. The most serious criticism comes from M. Kemp, "Looking at Leonardo's Last Supper" in *Appearance, Opinion, Change: Evaluating the Look of Paintings*, United Institute for Conservation, London 1990, and Id., "Authentically Dirty Pictures", in *The Times Literary Supplement*, 17 May 1991, to whom P.C. Marani replied in "Lettera a Martin Kemp (sul restauro del *Cenacolo*)" in *Raccolta Vinciana*, XXV, 1993, pp. 463–67. M. Kemp replied in turn to Marani in "Letter to Pietro Marani (on the Restoration of the *Last Supper*)," in *Raccolta Vinciana*, XXVI, 1995, pp. 359–66. See also J. Franck, "The Last Supper, 1497–1997: The Moment of Truth", in *Academia Leonardi Vinci. Journal of Leonardo Studies and Bibliography of Vinciana*, vol. X, 1997, pp. 165–82.

For the context and the critical reputation of *The Last Supper* from the sixteenth to the eighteenth centuries, see more recent works such as P.C. Marani, "Il Cenacolo di Leonardo e i suoi restauri nella Milano fra il XV e il XX secolo fra arte e fede, propaganda politica e magnificenza civile", in *I Tatti Studies: Essays in the Renaissance*, Volume 7 (1997), 1998, pp. 191–229. For the significance of the Eucharist to the painting and copies, see L. Steinberg, *Leonardo's Incessant Last Supper*, New York 2001; as well as the catalogue for the exhibition held at the Palazzo Reale in Milan in the same year: *Il Genio e le Passioni. Leonardo e il Cenacolo. Precedenti, innovazioni, riflessi di un capolavoro*, edited by P.C. Marani with a preface by Sir E. H. Gombrich, Milan 2001. In this last work the reader may find clarifications regarding the chronology of the various phases of the development of preliminary studies for the painting, slightly earlier than formerly believed, even as early as around 1490 (as is the case for the Windsor drawing no. 12542 discussed here); as well as speculation on the true identity of the patron who commissioned *The Last Supper* (possibly started on the initiative of Galeazzo Maria Sforza); and the critical reputation of the mural painting in the nineteenth and twentieth centuries. New information about the planning of the composition using a modular grid (a method later applied by Bramantino in his own works) has emerged from the most recent studies by Matthew Landrus which form the subject of his doctorate at Oxford University, and which the scholar himself relates in M. Landrus, "The Proportions of Leonardo's 'Last Supper'", in *Raccolta Vinciana*, vol. XXXII, pp.43–100. The importance and validity of the restoration of *The Last Supper* conducted by Pinin Brambilla have recently been acknowledged by Giovanni Romano as well; see his "Il restauro del Cenacolo di Leonardo: una nuova lettura", in *Il corpo dello stile. Cultura e lettura del restauro delle esperienze contemporanee. Studi in ricordo di Michele Cordaro*, edited by C. Piva and I. Sgarbozza, Bergamo-Rome 2005, pp. 53–64. Lastly, for the impact of *The Last Supper* on Leonardo's contemporaries up to Raphael, see P.C. Marani, "9 febbraio 1498: il Cenacolo svelato", in *I giorni di Milano*, Bari 2009.

The south wall of the refectory.
Giovanni Donato Montorfano
Crucifixion, 1495.
Fresco.

This large fresco occupies the wall opposite the *Last Supper*. It was a widespread tradition for the smaller side walls of monastery refectories to bear depictions of the *Crucifixion* and the *Last Supper*, and these two works were painted at almost the same time. The importance of Leonardo's masterpiece is such that its interesting companion piece tends to be somewhat overlooked. With its wealth of figures and descriptive detail, the scene is in a better state of preservation than Leonardo's work because Montorfano used the traditional fresco technique, which proves much more durable. The difference is made still more evident by comparison with the now almost entirely faded fresco-secco portraits of the family of Ludovico Sforza added on either side next to the groups of Dominican saints. The date 1495 and the signature of Montorfano are clearly identifiable on a tombstone by the feet of Mary Magdalene. This is indeed the only surviving work signed and dated by the artist, who was then at the end of his career. The composition follows the Lombard tradition with the figures arranged in groups around the crosses. Attention should be drawn in particular to the compact group of women on the left supporting Mary, a very popular motif in 15th-century Lombard painting and sculpture that can also be seen in the *Crucifixion* by Bramantino at Brera. The city of Jerusalem rises in the background from a rocky landscape that displays the influence of Paduan art. The "modern" architectural features of the buildings are practically a tribute to the style of Bramante, with whom Montorfano was in direct contact.